As My
Mother Would Say

As My Mother Would Say

Como Decia Mi Mama

JUDITH VALLES

AS MY MOTHER WOULD SAY
COMO DECIA MI MAMA

iUniverse books may be ordered through booksellers or by contacting:

iUniverse LLC
1663 Liberty Drive
Bloomington, IN 47403
www.iuniverse.com
1-800-Authors (1-800-288-4677)

ISBN: 978-1-4917-4437-6 (sc)
ISBN: 978-1-4917-4438-3 (e)

Library of Congress Control Number: 2014914476

Printed in the United States of America.

iUniverse rev. date: 08/12/2014

Preface

Have you ever wondered if there's an inner voice that you listen to when faced with a decision to make or a process to follow? I discovered mine by realizing that throughout my career in different positions I've had and under the different hats I've worn, I've cited my mother's proverbs or *dichos*.

I was raised in a conservative Mexican family that valued the traditions of Mexico. The proverbs or *dichos* were daily lessons from my mother. We believed that she made them up as situations arose—until we began using the *dichos* as adults, and other people from Mexico would laugh and say, "My grandma used to say that." These *dichos* are not so common anymore among young Mexican families.

My many friends, colleagues, coworkers, and students asked me to write these down because they found humor and common-sense advice in them, so I decided to do so. While some of these *dichos* may not sound sophisticated, profound, or intellectual, they have been invaluable to me, guiding me in my style of managing and leading.

Picture of Jovita Lopez de Valles

May, Mother's Day

I was sitting at the gravesite of my parents, and I found myself having a conversation with them as if they could hear me. I told them that I knew they would be proud of me, and I mourned the fact that my father died too young and my mother too ill to fully comprehend the impact their examples had on all of our lives. They would have been proud. I shared with them some of the events of my life and how even the tragic moments that I have suffered have made me a stronger and a more resilient woman. When opportunities came and doors opened, I entered them, feeling an overwhelming fear of failing. I did not want to disappoint those who believed in me, especially my mother. Her proverbs were ringing loudly in my mind. *Lo cortes, no quita lo valiente* (Courtesy does not take away your courage), *No des tu brazo a torcer* (Don't give up), *No hay mal que por bien no venga* (There is nothing bad that does not come from something good), and the list goes on and on.

There has not been a day that goes by that a situation does not automatically prompt a *dicho*. It came as a revelation when I realized that many decisions I have made in my life have been influenced by the *dichos* (sayings) of my mother.

As I reflected on my life, sitting at the graveside, my eyes became fixed on the dates on the graves of my parents, Gonzalo and Jovita. My father was forty-five when he died, and I realized that my mother was widowed when she was forty-two. I thought that was old then. She was left with eight children. I was seventeen at the time, and my oldest brother was twenty-nine. Yes, my mother was thirteen when she gave birth to my brother. Both of my parents were orphans in Mexico. They found comfort, love, support, and friendship in each other.

They ran away at the ages of twelve and fourteen. My father came to the United States at the age of fifteen, found a job, and then sent money to my mother so she could follow him. She entered the United States in 1922, at the age of thirteen and with a four-month-old baby.

(Photos taken October 29, 1922)

Their story is truly inspirational. They were courageous and determined. Both had a sixth-grade education, and they raised each other. My father was determined to learn English. He told my mother that the only way they would succeed in this country was to learn the language. With this in mind, he proceeded to teach himself by reading in English out loud every day.

They had eight children, and all of us but two received college degrees. My brothers and sisters were Antonio, Gonzalo, Francisco, Amilcar (Mike), Nohemi, Ruth, and Edith. Education was very important to my parents, especially to my mother. Since she was widowed at such a young age, she knew that we should not depend on others to bring us success or happiness; it was incumbent upon us to be prepared for life because one never knows what is in store.

They both would have been so proud when their daughter was elected to become the first Hispanic mayor of the city where they had chosen to raise their children and also the city where they had endured and suffered the pains of racism.

Racism against Mexicans has been documented in a book called *Not with the Fist*, written by Ruth Tuck in 1946. My father was an activist and organized a group of business leaders to sue the city for not allowing my oldest brother to attend a school where Mexicans were not allowed. In those days, the schools were part of the city's charter, and the charter called for "neighborhood" schools. That was changed as a result of this lawsuit. Another incident was when another brother of mine, Mike, was not allowed to swim in the city's swimming pool because Mexicans and blacks were allowed to use the pool only on Fridays, the day the pool was cleaned. Another incident involved my older brother, Gonzalo, who died during a training incident in the air force during World War II. His body was flown home. My parents wanted my brother to be buried by the Sacred Heart statue in our local cemetery. My father, who was fair skinned, made the initial contact and arrangements, and everything was fine until the cemetery officials saw my mother and asked if they were Mexican. The reply of course was affirmative. That's when the terrible blow came; my parents were told that Mexicans could not be buried at the spot my parents had selected.

His body was taken to our house, and I remember my brother's body lying in a coffin in our living room for what seemed like endless days. My father was not only furious but deeply offended, and he contacted our congressman, who was Harry Shepherd at that time. It was through the congressman's intervention that my brother was finally buried where my parents wanted him to be. The cemetery changed its policies.

My father died in 1951. Their courage has served as an example for all of us. After my father's death, my mother began studying English and enrolled in citizenship classes. She was so proud when she became a US citizen. There is not a day that goes by that I am not reminded of one of my mother's *dichos*. As an example, today I received a phone call from an acquaintance I had not heard from in months. I immediately said to myself, *"Solo cuando llueve y truena se acuerdan de Santa Elena"* (Only when it rains and thunders do they think of St. Elena). In other words, it is only when they need something that they remember me.

I thought my mother made these *dichos* up as situations arose, and quite honestly, I did not fully comprehend them as a child. However, as I grew up and was faced with different problems, adversities, and situations, one of my *jefa's dichos* would invariably pop up. *Jefa* is an endearing word for us that literally means *woman boss*, but for many of us raised in the barrio, it was also another word for mother.

Hence the purpose of this book: I have listed her *dichos* as I recall them. Throughout my career and adult life, I have always referred to her sayings by prefacing my comment with "as my mother used to say." It has usually taken place during certain situations with my students, coworkers, and colleagues over the years. The reaction from them has always been one of joy and amusement. They have all told me that I should write these down because they are priceless. I finally decided that I should. When I was studying for my master's degree in Spanish language and literature, I found many of my mother's sayings in works by Cervantes and Lope de Vega that describe the pride of the Spanish people as a possible detriment. I have attributed this to the fact that my mother's teachers were Catholic nuns, and they must have referred to the sayings in their classes.

In trying to capture the essence of my mother's wise *dichos*, I found it difficult to remember them in isolation. They come to me almost on a daily basis but in the context of the situations that arise. I found this out as I was trying to write all of them down.

On the following pages, I have written many of the *dichos* and different situations when they could be used. The literal translation to English may not make any sense. I will provide both the literal translation and the real meaning behind the words.

Dichos

Sayings and Literal Translations

1. *Lo cortes no quita lo valiente.* Courtesy does not take away courage.
2. *Mas vale pajaro en mano que cien volando.* A bird in the hand is worth more than a hundred flying.
3. *No niega la cruz de su parroquia.* He does not deny the cross of his parish.
4. *No hay mal que dure cien anos.* There is nothing bad that lasts a hundred years.
5. *No falta una chancla rota para una pata podrida.* There is always a torn slipper for a rotten foot.
6. *Bueno esta mi tata para mi nana.* My grandpa is fine for my grandma.

7. *No dejes para manana lo que puedas hacer hoy.* Don't leave for tomorrow what you can do today.

8. *A ti te lo digo mi hijo, entiendelo tu mi nuera.* I am telling you, my son; understand it, my daughter-in-law.

9. *Mejor que llore el solo hoy, y no tu con el manana.* Better he cries alone today than you cry with him tomorrow.

10. *Guarda tus lagrimas para cuando yo me muera.* Save your tears for when I die.

11. *No hay borracho que trague lumbre.* There is no drunk that will swallow fire.

12. *Enfermo que come y mea, el Diablo que ere lo crea.* A sick person who eats and urinates, only the devil will believe that he's sick.

13. *Esta como los musicos malos, entran y salen a mear.* He is like a bad musician, coming and going to "pee."

14. *El hambre me tumba y el orgullo me levanta.* Hunger knocks me down, but pride lifts me up.

15. *Esta como el caballo del Espanol, cuando aprendio a no comer, se murio.* He's

like the Spaniard's horse; just when he learned not to eat, he died.

16. *No hay que decir "ape" hasta que no escape.* One must not say "ape" until you escape.

17. *Dime con quien andas, y te dire quien eres.* Tell me who you hang around with, and I'll tell you who you are.

18. *Mas sabe el diablo por viejo que por Diablo.* The devil knows more because he's old and not because he's the devil.

19. *Le dieron gato por liebre.* They gave him a cat for a hare.

20. *Lo barato cuesta caro.* Cheap things cost more.

21. *Anda como ronron, de aprontona.* She's like a beetle purring around looking for attention or a tasty place to land.

22. *La verdad no peca pero incomoda.* The truth does not sin, but it creates discomfort.

23. *Viste al mono, para que otra lo baile.* She dresses the monkey so another woman will dance him around.

24. *Las apariencias enganan.* Appearances are deceiving.

25. *No des tu brazo a torcer.* Don't let your arm be bent.

26. *No le busques tres pies al gato, ya sabes que tiene cuatro.* Don't look for three legs on a cat; you know it has four.

27. *Mas vale viejo por conocido que nuevo por conocer.* There is more value in the old and known than the new and unknown.

28. *Hijo de gato, gatito, hija de gata, gatita.* Son of a male cat, male kitty, daughter of a female cat, female kitty.

29. *Cae mas pronto un hablador que un cojo.* A loudmouth or a braggart trips faster than a person who limps.

30. *Busca trabajo, pidiendole a Dios, no encontrar.* He is looking for work and praying to God not to find any.

31. *El flojo y el mezquino, anda dos veces el camino.* A stingy man and a lazy man walk the road twice.

32. *Lo del agua al agua.* That which is water goes to water.

33. *Tiene cuerpo de tentacion y cara de arrepentimiento.* She has a tempting body but a face of regret.

34. *Como te ves, me vi; como me ves te veras.*
As I see you, I saw myself; as you see
me, you will see yourself.

35. *Arrieros somos y en el camino andamos.*
We are all mule drivers, and we are on
the same road.

36. *Nadie se va de este mindo sin pagar las
que debe.* No one leaves this world
without paying what he owes.

37. *No hay mal que por bien no venga.* There
is nothing bad that does not come from
something good.

38. *Primero mis dientes, despues mis parientes.*
First my teeth, then my relatives.

39. *Este huevo quiere sal.* This egg wants
salt.

40. *De favor te abrazan, y quieres que te
aprieten.* They hug you as a favor, and
you want them to squeeze you.

41. *Enojense las comadres, y saquense las
verdades.* When the godmothers get
angry, the truth comes out.

42. *Se ahoga en un vaso de agua.* He drowns
in a glass of water.

43. *Todo cabe en un jarrito, sabiendolo acomodar.* Everything fits in a little jar, if you know how to arrange it.

44. *En la tierra del ciego, el tuerto es rey.* In the land of the blind, the one-eyed person is king.

45. *Le dieron la carne al diablo, y ahora le dan los huesos a Dios.* They gave the meat to the devil, and now they give the bones to God.

46. *Cada loco con su tema, y cada chango su mecate.* Every crazy man with his topic and every monkey with his rope.

47. *De un piojo hacen un caballero.* They make a gentleman out of a louse (or head lice).

48. *El comal le dijo a la olla.* A skillet said to the pot.

49. *Ojos que no ven, corazon que no siente.* Eyes that don't see won't feel pain in their heart.

50. *En boca cerrada, no entran moscas.* Flies don't enter a closed mouth.

51. *Aunque el mono se vista de seda, mono se queda.* A monkey may be dressed in silk, but it is still a monkey.

52. *Mejor sola que mal acompanada.* It's better to be alone than with a bad companion.

53. *La educacion no se aprende, se mama.* Education is not learned; it is suckled or nursed at your mother's breast.

Dichos de La Jefa
(My mother's sayings)

Translations and Situational Applications and Uses

1. *Lo cortes no quita lo valiente.*

This *dicho* has been invaluable to me during my entire professional career. The words ring in my ears every day, especially during trying times with difficult people. The translation says it all: "Courtesy does not take away courage." In other words, maintain your composure, and there is no need for harsh words or expletives. Bite your tongue, and be a master of the unspoken word.

2. *Mas vale pajaro en mano que cien volando.*

The translation of this says it all: "Better to have a bird in your hand than one hundred birds flying." Go for the sure thing.

3. *No niega la cruz de su parroquia.*

La jefa would say this when describing a person's looks or behavior. Translation: "He (or she) cannot deny the cross of his (or her) parish." In other words, he or she looks or behaves just like his or her relatives or parents.

4. *No hay mal que dure cien anos.*

Translation: "There is nothing bad that will last a hundred years." In other words, this will pass. No need to fret over the matter, whatever is.

5. *No faltara una chancla rota para una pata podrida.*

Translation: "There is always a torn slipper for a rotten foot." This would refer to an unusual couple or a pair where one would think neither could ever find a mate for one reason or another. This is usually used to describe a couple whose personalities or looks are not enviable.

6. *Bueno esta mi tata para mi nana.*

Translation: "My grandpa is fine for my grandma." This expression is used when a couple complements each other for better or for worse in looks and/or behavior.

7. *No dejes para manana lo que puedes hacer hoy.*

Translation: "Don't leave for tomorrow what you can do today." The use of this saying is obvious. Mom would say this to keep us from procrastinating. She believed in taking care of things as they came up and not leaving them for another day.

8. *A ti te lo digo mi hijo entiendelo tu mi nuera.*

Translation: "I am speaking to you, my son, and I hope my daughter-in-law 'gets it.'" This describes a mother-in-law when giving unsolicited advice to the son, but the words and advice are really intended for the other listener. You don't have to be a mother-in-law to do this.

9. *Mejor que llore el solo y no tu con el manana.*

Translation: "Better that he cries alone today and not you cry with him tomorrow (in the future)." She would say this to me when I had to scold one of my children, and they would begin to cry. If I would soften, she would remind me that it is better for the child to cry alone today so that I would not cry with them tomorrow. *Tienen que ser bien educados.* They must be well educated;

the real discipline and education is up to the parents. *Mal educado* is the opposite of *bien educado*. Education in the Spanish sense is being well mannered and courteous.

10. *Guarda tus lagrimas para cuando me muera.*

Translation: "Save your tears for when I die." What she meant by this was that real tears should not be wasted on minor things and some pain. In other words, don't sweat the small stuff.

11. *No hay borracho que trague lumbre.*

Translation: "There is not a drunk that will swallow fire."

She would say this when someone made excuses for a person that was acting stupid or saying inappropriate things, saying that he or she had too much to drink and was not responsible for whatever distasteful actions they have been engaged in or said. This *dicho* says that they *are* aware of what they say and do. A drunk's behavior is usually indicative of his or her real character.

12. *Enfermo que come y mea, el Diablo que se lo crea*.

Translation: "A sick person who eats and urinates, only the devil will believe him." This is used when it appears that someone is pretending to be sick for one reason or another but has a healthy appetite and no problems going potty.

13. *Esta como los musicos malos, entran y salen a mear*.

Translation: "He is like a bad musician, coming and going to 'pee,' because he does not know the music as well as he should." This would be used for workers who spend more time going in and out, taking breaks, and making excuses instead of doing the job.

14. *El hambre me tumba y el orgullo me levanta.*

Translation: "Hunger knocks me down, but pride lifts me up."
This *dicho* is reflective of Spanish pride. Mother would say this rather than giving up, conceding, or making excuses.

15. *Esta como el caballo del Espanol; cuando aprendio a no comer, se murio.*

Translation: "He is like the Spaniard's horse; just when he was learning not to eat, he died." This *dicho* is used to describe someone's exaggerated sense of pride and often times to the detriment of the person involved.

16. *No ay que decir "ape" hasta que no escape.*

Translation: "One must not say 'ape' until you escape." In other words, don't count your chickens until they hatch.

17. *Dime con quien andas, y te dire quien eres.*

This was her way of monitoring our friends. Translation: "Tell me who you hang around with, and I'll tell you who you are."

18. *Mas sabe el diablo por viejo que por Diablo.*

Translation: "The devil knows more because he's old and not because he is the devil." In other words, there is wisdom from older folks, so listen up and learn!

19. *Le dieron gato por liebre.*

Translation: "They gave him a cat instead of a rabbit." When a cat is skinned, it looks just like a skinned rabbit. This is an expression used when someone cheats you out of something or sells you a fake for the real thing.

20. *Lo barato cuesta caro.*

Translation: "Cheap things cost more in the long run."

21. *Anda como ronron de aprontona.*

Translation: "He or she is like a beetle purring around looking for attention or something." That person is always in your face.

22. *La verdad no peca, pero incomoda.*

Translation: "The truth does not sin, but it creates discomfort."

23. *Viste al mono para que otra lo baile.*

Translation: "She dresses the monkey so that another will dance him around." Used to describe a woman who takes pride in her husband's looks and attire and makes sure that his clothes are clean and well pressed; he is known by all to be a womanizer.

24. *Las apariencias enganan.*

Translation: "Looks are deceiving."

25. *No des tu brazo a torcer.*

Translation: "Don't allow your arm to be bent." In other words, don't give up.

26. *No le busques tres pies al gato ya sabes que tiene cuatro.*

Translation: "Don't look for three legs on the cat; you know it has four." Don't question the obvious, especially when it is clear that you know the answer. You may be stirring up trouble.

27. *Mas vale viejo por conocido que nuevo por conocer.*

Translation: "There is more value in the old and known than the new of which you have no knowledge." In other words, go for the tried and true rather than the new and unknown.

28. *Hijo de gato ... gatito (hija de gata ... gatita).*

Translation: "Son of a male cat is a little male kitty, daughter of a female cat is a little female kitty." In other words: What do you expect? Look at the parents.

29. *Cae mas pronto un hablador que un cojo.*

Translation: "A loudmouth or a braggart trips faster than a person who limps." In other words, all show and no go.

30. *Busca trabajo, pidiendole a Dios no encontrar.*

Translation: "He is looking for work and praying to God not to find any."

31. *El flojo y el mezquino, anda dos veces el camino.*

Translation: "A lazy man and a stingy man walk the path twice." In other words, it takes a lazy man or a stingy man twice as long to get something done.

32. *Lo del agua al agua.*

Translation: "What is from water becomes water." In other words: don't fret over spilled water … get over it.

33. *Tiene cuerpo de tentacion y cara de arrepentimiento.*

Translation: "She has a body of temptation and a face of regret." In other words, she has a great body, but her face doesn't complement it. As the young people say, she has a "butter face."

34. *Como te ves, me vi; como me ves, te veras.*

Translation: "As I see you, I saw myself; as you see me, you will see yourself."

35. *Arrieros somos y en el camino andamos.*

Translation: "We are mule drivers, and we're on the road."

In other words, we are the same. All of us are on the same road, walking, driving, or pushing one thing or another.

36. *Nadie se va de este mundo, sin pagar las que debe.*

Translation: "No one leaves this world without paying what you owe." Used as a word of caution not to cause harm or do anything that you know is wrong because it will come back to bite you.

37. *No hay mal que por bien no venga.*

Translation: "There is nothing bad that does not come from something good." Used to explain that there is a good reason why something is happening. Learn from it.

38. *Primeros mis dientes, despues, mis parientes.*

Translation: "First my teeth and then my relatives." Take care of yourself first and then the rest. First things first.

39. *Este huevo quiere sal.*

Translation: "This egg wants salt." Used to describe someone that wants something from you and disguises it by flattering you.

40. *De favor te abrazan, y quieres que te aprieten.*

Translation: "They are embracing you as a favor, and you want them to hug you tighter." When someone does you a favor, be grateful and don't ask for more.

41. *Enojense las comadres y saquense las verdades.*

Translation: "When the godmothers get mad, the truth comes out." People will tell all when they are angry with anyone, relatives or former friends.

42. *Se ahoga en un vaso de agua.*

Translation: "He drowns in a glass of water." Everything is doom and gloom.

43. *Todo cabe en un jarrito, sabiendolo acomodar.*

Translation: "Everything fits in a little jar, if you know how to arrange it as you are putting it in." This expression is used when you are trying to organize and are putting things away.

44. *En la tierra del ciego, el tuerto es rey.*

Translation: "In the land of the blind, the one-eyed person is king." A person with a little knowledge about something appears to be wise, especially when no one else is familiar with the topic.

45. *Le dieron la carne al diablo y ahora le dan los huesos a Dios.*

Translation: "They gave the meat to the devil, and now they are giving the bones to God." Mom would say this about pious people in church who were real hell-raisers in their youth and now are holier than thou in their senior years.

46. *Cada loco con su tema, y cada chango su mecate.*

Translation: "Every crazy man with his topic, and every monkey with his rope." In other words: everyone does his or her own thing.

47. *De un piojo hacen un caballero.*

Translation: "They make a gentleman out of a louse." In other words, they are prone to hyperbole.

48. *El comal le dijo a la olla.*

Similar to the pot calling the kettle black. A *comal* is a flat skillet used to cook tortillas, and an *olla* is a pot.

49. *Ojos que no ven, corazon que no siente.*

Similar to: what you don't know won't hurt you. She used this as advice to others who were prone to meddle in other's personal or family affairs.

50. *En boca cerrada, no entran moscas.*

Translation: "Flies don't enter a closed mouth." Used when someone talks too much and puts their foot in their mouth. Similar to being a master of the unspoken word and not a slave to the spoken one.

51. *Aunque el mono se vista de seda, mono se queda.*

Translation: "You may dress a monkey in silk, but it is still a monkey." This expression was used by my mother to describe a person who dressed in very expensive clothes or had an impressive title but had no class.

52. *Mejor sola que mal acompanada.*

Translation: "It is better to be alone than with someone who is a bad influence or toxic."

53. *La educacion no se aprende, se mama.*

Translation: "Education is not learned; it is suckled or nursed by your mother's breast." Education in the Spanish sense refers to being courteous, polite, and well mannered. That is a person *bien educado*. It does not refer to the degrees earned, but to the person's behavior. A classy person is *bien educado*.

Gonzalo and Jovita Valles, 1946

About the Author

Judith Valles made history when she became the first Latina president of a college or university in the state of California in 1988. After she retired from a successful career in education, where she began as an elementary teacher and ended as a college president, she made history again by becoming the first Hispanic mayor of her city of San Bernardino in 1998, and the first female Hispanic mayor of any city in the United States with more than 100,000 residents. She currently serves on several boards, conducts leadership workshops and seminars, and is often sought as a speaker. She lives in San Bernardino, California. She attributes her achievements to the examples and teachings of her parents.

www.ingramcontent.com/pod-product-compliance
Lightning Source LLC
Chambersburg PA
CBHW030545290526
45786CB00004B/1869